By The Grace

Grace

A True Story Of

Triumph Over Trauma

Brianna Spinuzzi

By The Grace

Printed in the United States Of America.

Edited by Alisha Leslie

First Printing 2025

ISBN 9798243431071

Storyline Publishing

PO Box 504 Broomfield, CO. 80038

Dedicated to our Lord God for showing me

grace and blessing me again and again.

Also, to my beautiful little family and all their

support. - I love you forever.

A Letter To The Readers

This book has been a passion project of mine ever since I took part in an emotional and life-changing Bible study.

Like a lot of women, my story involves trauma and heartbreak. Many of the pangs I went through are topics people don't like to discuss but bringing light to them was exactly what I needed. That, and God.

I kept my story a secret from almost everyone and turned away from God, ashamed. After hitting rock bottom and unable to bury it any longer, I turned to my Creator for healing.

What I found nearly broke me, but it also built me up. I have never felt closer or more connected to God and I want more than anything for others to experience the same.

It is by the grace of God that I have found myself, a purpose and most importantly, HIM!

It is my hope that anyone who reads this will be inspired to share their story with others and find grace in our good, good, God.

Contents

1. Growing Up Christian

2. To Love And To Lose

3. Strength Is Beauty

4. Storm Clouds

5. The Twelve-Year Night

6. Fast Forward

7. Swan Song

8. Where There's A Will

9. The Weight Of It All

10. Our Story In The Stars

11. In The Shadows

12. The Mountains Are Calling

13. Now I'm Found

14. By The Grace

Preface

Something inside me snapped. A chord had been struck and all I could think about was how uncertain I was about my eternal life. Not because I didn't have faith but because my past had suddenly become a dark cloud over everything I thought I knew. I had lost the ability to believe I was worthy. The weight of what I had done felt far too heavy for any kind of redemption. My mind was racing with thoughts of my children and how I had failed them; how despite all my efforts to point them to Jesus, I myself might not join them at His side after leaving this world.

Thankfully, and with all credit to the Lord, those thoughts were put to rest;

though not before enduring a long and painful journey to rediscover God and everything I had seemingly forgotten. While painful and messy, my journey has led me to fully embrace His grace and be grateful for the path that led me here. Learning to accept what once was and appreciate where you are now is something to be valued. The very story that once left me speechless and hidden from the Lord, is now the very story that has inspired me to help others achieve the closeness and pure gratitude I feel toward God and everything He's written for my life.

Growing Up Christian

I grew up in a Christian household and I've believed in God for as long as I can remember. We attended church every Easter and Christmas at the very least, and more frequently when we were able to find a good church.

As a child, my mistakes and sins would devastate me and I'd hold onto them for a long time. I still remember being torn up over the fact that I had "tagged" the sidewalk in front of our elementary school with crayon. I lost sleep thinking I had done something that I shouldn't have.

While I was a daydreamer and often as my Mom said, in 'la-la land', I remember being very concerned about people that were less fortunate as well as those that endured war. For several years in a row, I blew out my birthday candles wishing for "world peace". When my dad learned this, he encouraged me to wish for something for myself. He wanted to preserve my innocence and childhood and I had yet to learn that something of that magnitude would take far more than a birthday wish.

Also, at an early age I rephrased my bedtime prayers to say "we", instead of "I", feeling insensitive to pray for my salvation alone. I was very in tune with my spirituality and I took prayers and compassion for others seriously.

When I was about nine years old, I saw an angel while worshiping at church. I watched in awe as a faint glow surrounding one of the women on stage floated into the air and drifted away, their wings waving. Never really knowing what it meant, I forgot about it for a long time. Going through everything I did, I thought of that day in church and smiled, knowing there was a reason. I believe God wanted me to foster that feeling in my heart and soul and never let it fade; to hold onto that childlike innocence and unwavering faith.

Our parents raised us right and taught us all the values that should be instilled in children at a young age. Family is important to each of us and the deep connections we had as children have amplified as adults. My siblings, parents, and I have great relationships with one another and the importance of that has transferred to our own parenting values.

I was the third of six children and exemplified the typical "middle child" characteristics. A sense of not belonging and unsure where I fit in, I often felt a desire to run away. My attempts were always short lived and quickly forgotten but the feeling remained a constant for many years to follow. I strived to succeed and prove my abilities while also rebelling in an attempt to gain some independence.

"Forget regret or life is yours to miss" was my senior quote in the yearbook. While that young, 'once upon a time' version of me was naive and yet to experience any real regret, I was on to something. I have absolutely done things I regret. Case in point, the night that changed me forever. Equally regretful, how I handled the situation. However, I still have a hard time truly regretting the choices I've made and experiences I've been through. Without them, I might not be where I am spiritually.

I spent the entirety of my twenties struggling to take care of and find myself. Moving from one apartment to another, job to job, mistake after mistake, I fumbled to make a name for myself. Somewhere along the line, I began to stray from God and what He wanted for me. Losing sight of who He was and who I was, I made choices based on how I was feeling, rather than what was right or true. Surrounding myself with people who made poor choices and dating people who were completely wrong for me.

Do not be deceived. "Bad company ruins good morals" 1 Cor 15:33

I often dated people for who they were as a person, not who I was. It's easy to become consumed by the presence of a person in your life; the way you see them and the way they make you feel, the good qualities that they possess and the future you wish for. While it's great to see the best in people, I have learned through many relationships that you cannot make that a precedence over what you see in yourself. More importantly, what God has planned for you.

Although I grew up as a Christian and have believed in His creation and vast greatness for as long as I can remember, my life has not always mirrored that. Somewhere on the path to find myself, I lost God. Ironically, but by no surprise, that's when I struggled the most. I was surrounded by people but all alone, smiling constantly but not able to find *true* joy.

To Love And To Lose

I believe I was fortunate to love and be loved so many times. Each relationship and person taught me something different about myself or the world.

My first serious relationship inspired my love for adventure and the outdoors. Going out of my comfort zone quickly *became* my comfort zone. Our connection was based on doing things I had never done before, usually a hobby of his. I went along for the ride and uncovered my own need for adventure. Despite our shared interest in a life of fun, some of our core values did not align and I began to feel like I was losing my own identity.

True to form, I fell quickly into a new relationship. He was incredibly kind and funny and the type of guy that attracts a lot of attention. We had been working together and gotten to know each other pretty well. Falling hard and fast, we moved in together after just a few months and were together for a couple of years. Although I believe we truly loved one another, we began to lose respect for each other and our relationship, both behaving in ways we shouldn't have. A lot of people asked what went wrong and there was no real explanation other than we just weren't right for each other.

I was in one more long-term relationship before dating my husband. That relationship was probably the most controversial because we were two *very* different people. None of our values or interests seemed to align but something pulled us together, more than once. While a lot of people were blinded by who he was on paper, I saw something in him; he had this intense loyalty about him and he would've walked through fire for me. Much of who he was changed while we were together and I know he would've bent over backward to be who I needed but I didn't want to change him. I just wanted to find "The One", the person whom my soul spoke to.

As fate would have it and as God so perfectly planned, my husband and I found one another. Our relationship was tested and had its ups and downs but everything we went through only made us more resilient. We became an even stronger team and knew that without a doubt, our paths were meant to cross. I am grateful for everything we went through and where it led us today; happily married with four beautiful children.

I have no regrets about the amount of times I've loved, nor the fact that I was so willing to share my heart. My belief is that life is meant to be shared with people you love and I've been fortunate enough to experience that multiple times. Nonetheless, I wish I hadn't compromised my relationship with Jesus while on the path to find love. Loving others and sharing your thoughts and dreams with those closest to you is not the problem.

Allowing yourself to be blinded by those feelings is where the danger lies; to love someone else but to lose yourself.

Looking back on my life and the choices I made, I'm unable to pinpoint when it happened. When did my mission to find myself become a journey spent walking someone else's path? At what point did I forget what's important? The only real way to find yourself and unveil your purpose is to build intimacy with God himself. No other being on earth can help you know yourself like He can.

Whoever finds their life will lose it, and whoever loses their life for my sake will find it. Matthew 10:39

For many years, I believed I was the black sheep of my family and not because I was told so, but because I labeled myself as such. A self-proclaimed black sheep. Developing a complex like that at an early age made me think of myself as an outsider. I felt as though I had a different outlook on life and because I didn't follow in the footsteps of my sisters, I was the odd one out. Dancing to the beat of my own drum, I was always a wanderer, doing things my own way and often learning the hard way. Truthfully, the voice inside my head that created this complex became really loud. It was as though I was convinced that if it was conventional and expected in any way, it wasn't *my* way.

Extremely passionate and outspoken with my feelings, I followed my heart every time. Like a lot of people, I used my heart as a compass and went in the direction of whatever made me happy. God, however, doesn't always wish for us to be happy and following your heart can lead you down a dangerous path. Often we confuse our happiness, even the temporary or false, as a sign that we are following God's path and doing as His will suggests. While God has big plans for us, He doesn't always intend for us to be happy, rather we find happiness in following His word and achieving it as a result of putting our faith in His plan.

Trust in the Lord with all your heart, and do not lean on your own understanding. Proverbs 3:5

I have no remorse for choosing to live outside of the societal "norm" but I do regret following my heart and not Jesus. Choosing to take my happiness into my own hands instead of letting Jesus lead me was the first and most crucial mistake of my youth.

Following anything or anyone other than Jesus will never lead you to where you're meant to be. In trying to discover who I was and what I was meant to be, I only wound up more lost. No matter how hard I tried, my efforts always fell short because I wasn't navigating the dark with Him as my light.

Looking back, there were so many times that I desperately needed my Savior and instead of turning to Him for answers, I found them elsewhere. What I found only drove me further away from Him. I wish so badly that I would've kept up a dialogue with Him during those years and those times that I needed Him most.

All we like sheep have gone astray; we have turned— every one—to his own way; and the Lord has laid on him the iniquity of us all. Isaiah 53:6

Some people have to be pulled under the waves, turning their lives completely upside down before they can truly understand the power of the rushing water. Although I hate to admit it, I have proved to be one of those people again and again.

Strength Is Beauty

As a young girl, I remember envying those that had struggled in life. A weird concept I know, but there was something so admirable about someone who had gone through the lowest of lows and found a way to rise above. Even at a young age and prior to any real struggles of my own, I could see that they had such an appreciation for life as well as a confident sense of who they were.

Thinking often about the many people in the world who were less fortunate than us plagued me and forced me to believe I didn't deserve such a wonderful life. Up until and after having my own children, I would think "What have *I* done to be worthy of such great blessings?" It was as though I was always waiting for the other shoe to drop.

I always thought I was pretty strong, capable of enduring a good amount. My mom told me once that "God only gives us what we can handle" and I held on tight to that reminder every time I experienced something painful or confusing.

And the Lord will guide you continually and satisfy your desire in scorched places and make your bones strong; and you shall be like a watered

garden, like a spring of water, whose waters do not fail. Isaiah 58:11

I told myself so many times that there was beauty in strength and that my story held no weight in comparison to others. Often when I'm going through something tough or struggling to keep my emotions at bay, I quickly snap myself out of it by remembering that things could be much worse.

While sometimes that's true and it's good to allow yourself an opportunity to see that perspective, it's also very unhealthy. When we refuse to address how we're feeling because we minimize the pain or emotion, we're really only putting it off or pushing it down. In other words, it *will* come up later and it will affect you when you least expect it.

Yes, someone has possibly experienced something more traumatic than what you're currently upset about, but that doesn't mean you aren't allowed to feel your feelings. We are human and designed to feel a wide array of emotions. Denying our hearts to feel those is denying our souls the chance to grieve and grow, mourn and move on. We must go through the process of feeling every emotion that comes up because it is with great necessity that those feelings were put on our soul.

It's not surprising that so many people struggle with mental health, especially in a world that can be so devastatingly crushing. When we don't allow ourselves to process what we need to, it becomes impossible to ever advance our understanding of the cards we've been dealt. It is for a reason that we must go through what we do; God has put that in our path so we may grow and help others do the same.

Also being overly optimistic, I think I've handled some serious and intense situations with very little caution. I wasn't careful to take the time to grieve as I should've. I didn't allow myself to feel the pain or anger that I needed in order to heal properly. My healing was surface-level and lacked the level of care that it deserved.

Twelve and a half years later, I still hadn't handled my experience properly. Not seeking therapy or consulting with anyone, I kept trying to deal with it on my own.

There are several times in the Bible where we read about Jesus coming to heal the broken and God's immeasurable grace. Both are excellent reminders for people like myself that have been through something that brings them shame or regret.

We've all been through something or *multiple* things that have shook us to the core and made us question our own worthiness. The Bible however, speaks of how *we* are the ones that Jesus came to save.

And when Jesus heard it, he said to them, "Those who are well have no need of a physician, but those who are sick. I came not to call the righteous, but sinners."
Mark 2:17

Coincidentally, the night that changed me forever, I had been showing friends my newest tattoo that reads "Strength Is Beauty". I chose to get it on my ribs as I wanted the placement to mean as much as the phrase itself; there is beauty to be found in being strong. Little did I know I was about to need that reminder more than ever.

Storm Clouds

It seemed like an entirely different life and a completely different person that had been through the experience. I quickly buried all the pain, shame and my memory of important details in an attempt to forget it had ever happened. Of course, my mind clung tight to the imagery and feelings. Closing my eyes, I am able to go right back to the night that changed me forever. Even the cliff note version of everything I went through was enough to destroy me every time I revisited that moment in time.

I spent so much of my life just "getting by" as a Christian. Believing whole-heartedly in God but "silently" sinning. Claiming I was a Christian but behaving in ways that would suggest otherwise. I had considered myself a *mostly* good person but suddenly I was questioning every decision I ever made, fearful that I had sealed my fate.

As a mother, I am always a little anxious about the world our children are growing up in. Equally, I'm always worried about how badly we will screw them up because of our own, unaddressed baggage. Still, this seemed to be more than that. I was deep in thought about our lives beyond this world and truly believed I was going to hell for what I did. Thinking for one second that I could possibly be separated from my creator and all the people I love was eating me up inside.

Suddenly paralyzed by the memories, I couldn't spend a minute alone without the harrowing thoughts creeping in. My husband continued to say "You did what you had to do, I support you and how you handled it." Unfortunately, his words would only comfort me for a short time before I went right back to that dark place where I hated myself for what happened and what I had done. It began to consume my thoughts and emotions on a daily basis and I couldn't see past it anymore. As far down as I attempted to bury the pain, I could no longer avoid the obvious distress that lingered in my heart and in my mind.

Although he tried, it was difficult for my husband to truly understand my emotional struggles. He offered as many kind words and support as he could, but he felt helpless in attempting to console me. Although we already dated for almost two and a half years, we weren't together at the time of the incident. In fact, I believe the pain of our breakup was a catalyst for everything that happened that dreadful night. Even so, I still felt comfortable telling him *most* of the story shortly after it happened. I confided in him about what I had been through and all the emotions that came with it. I felt seen and heard and he never judged me.

If you ever break up with someone and they handle your heart with the same tenderness as they did before, that says

more about their character than anything.

Thankfully, we found our way back together and have now been married for almost ten years. Even when he doesn't know exactly what to say or do to make me feel better, he has always shown me love and kindness when I needed it most. His faith in me and the strength I possess helped me to believe more in myself. Regrettably though, even the most tender of hearts can't mend a heart that is broken by shame and self-hatred.

I also spoke with my mom about the pain and flooded emotions that suddenly resurfaced. I was living with my parents for a couple of months during that time, so she was by my side every step of the way. Offering her love and support, she was there to comfort me as I curled up in my bed, crying and confused. Her words of compassion were similar to those of my husband, trying to ensure me that I did what I had to.

Without effectively grieving loss or handling trauma, eventually our past will resurface. Twelve and a half years later, I found myself struggling to breathe as mine caught up with me. As the pain from my past began to interfere with my ability to think about anything else, I knew it was time to address all the emotions that I hadn't before. It was time to face the truth and all the nightmares that came with it. It was time to *finally* turn to God.

My husband approached me and said he had found something that I could benefit from-a Bible study for women in healing. God had answered my unspoken prayers for desperately wanting to face this demon and He used my husband as a messenger.

Excited about the prospect of moving on from the pain, I was eager to reach out to the woman coordinating the Bible study. Getting up the courage to actually attend however, took several months and the additional push from someone who watched me go through it. The first time I attempted to take part in the group, I became anxious about what I'd be walking into and couldn't bring myself to go. Finally though, after hitting rock bottom, I knew I needed help and that I wasn't going to get through this pain and suffering without the support from women who had experienced something similar.

Walking into the Bible study felt like I was walking into a courtroom; I was up in arms about protecting myself and anxious for other people to hear the truth. Expecting the worst but hoping for the best, my emotions were right at the surface. I cried the entire first session of our Bible study, uncomfortably and uncontrollably for two hours. It was obvious to the other women there that I had some serious baggage and was very emotional about discussing it.

Knowing what I know now, it's hard to imagine I could've ever believed I was destined to go to Hell. It makes me sad to think how far down that hole I went but going through trauma does that to you. It robs you of many things, but the worst for me was my loss of faith, in myself as well as in God.

The Twelve-Year Night

My heart was broken. My now husband and I had broken up after over two years together. It was the kind of breakup that's brought on by poor timing and agendas, not a loss of love. Although neither of us really wanted it, we needed it.

I was living at home for a few months and working yet *another* restaurant job that I hated. Disappointed about the way things turned out and feeling lost, I tried to escape. One night I went to dinner with a group of friends and their significant others. The company, while good, only made me feel worse about my current situation.

After everyone left, I went to meet up with a friend for some drinks. A friend of hers was having people over so the two of us went there. The host was a guy we hung out with before but I didn't care for him. I thought he was pompous and self-righteous; the type of guy who prides himself on winning girls over. Every other time we had been in the same room, I was with my boyfriend and easily ignored him.

On this particular night, everything was different. I was extremely forward with him and acted unlike myself, openly flirting with him in front of people I barely knew. Memories of that night paint me as this unrestrained, uncharacteristic version of myself. We had been drinking so I used that as an excuse for my behavior, feeling ashamed at how easily I let my inhibitions go. Looking back, that detail floods my brain and every single time, I have stopped myself from seeing anything other than my carelessness. The level of blame I placed on myself is a direct response to everything that followed.

He took my hand and led me up the stairs to his bedroom. That one line destroys me every time it leaves my mouth or finds the paper. Never have such few words held so much weight and pain.

From that moment on, my memory went black. I don't remember a single thing that transpired from the minute he grabbed my hand to the walk up the stairs, or anything thereafter. That is, until I came to for a brief second. We were lying in his bed, his body wrapped around me. I was conscious long enough to realize that he was inside me before my memory failed me again. When I woke again, the same scenario replayed, only it was now morning.

As soon as it was over, I frantically searched for my clothes and rushed to the bathroom. Unaware at the time what just happened, the only thing I could think of was how embarrassed I'd be to run into his roommate in the hall. His roommate was actually a nice guy and I had suspected he liked me though the feeling wasn't mutual. I was concerned that he'd see me leaving the room and it might hurt his feelings.

Embarrassment and guilt. Those were the first two things that came to mind. It's obvious now that I had no clue what I just experienced.

Luckily, I hadn't fully processed the night (or morning) because I had to ask him for a ride to my car. The drive was awkward and incredibly uncomfortable but it would've been much worse had I understood that I just got in the car with a predator.

I felt uneasy and confused but simply labeled it as him taking advantage of my vulnerability. Never, for over twelve years, did I tell anyone exactly how the night unfolded and for over twelve years, I myself, didn't realize what happened.

My mind went straight to a state of regret and blame. Not towards him, but towards myself; for being in a situation where I could possibly lose control, for drinking too much and for being too forward. I even went to the extreme of attempting to date him afterwards. This sounds a lot like Stockholm syndrome as I say this, but I tried to justify what happened. Similar to victims of abuse or captivity, I made excuses for him and avoided any alibi that painted me as a victim. I convinced myself that we slept together and that having a one-night stand wouldn't be so terrible if we were dating. Describing to my friends what happened that night, I just said "I drank too much and we slept together."

It should come as no shock that I quickly discovered my initial intuitions about the guy were correct. After going on two dates and turning him down each time, we eventually stopped talking. Just like that, we cut ties. No accountability was taken and no repercussions were made on his part.

Moving forward, I did my best to forget that night ever happened. Naive and stubborn, I saw that night as nothing more than a mistake on my part. I marked it as a bad date and promised myself to avoid anyone like him in the future.

You know how they say "When it rains, it pours"? The series of events that happened that night and the next couple of months felt more like a tsunami.

A few weeks after that night, I was hit by another car as I was driving home. She turned left and hit me as I was driving through a green light. Had I not seen her at the last minute and hit the brakes suddenly, she most likely would've T-boned me right in the driver-side door. Not a single person stopped to check on either of us and once the police responded to my call, they were equally unhelpful. She insisted her light was green and because there were no witnesses to say otherwise, they found us both at fault. Fortunately, neither of us were seriously hurt, just shaken up.

Three days later, on my now husband's birthday, I received what felt like the worst possible news. After getting sick that morning and hesitantly taking a test, I discovered I was pregnant.

Everything went black again. I couldn't believe what was happening. That was *one* night. One night that I didn't want. One night that I tried to forget.

Fast Forward

Unlike all the times I've gotten a positive pregnancy test since, my future felt confusing and scary, not grateful or blessed. I don't think I really allowed myself to feel anything. I shut down emotionally. As someone who is extremely sensitive and tends to wear their heart on their sleeve(and emotions on her face), that was something I had never experienced. Never in my life had I been able to put my emotions aside and ignore what I was feeling.

Thinking about that day years later, my heart sinks every time. That was one of the most traumatizing moments in my life;

both the night it happened, as well as reading the test. Yet, I cannot for the life of me remember feeling anything other than shock. A wave of cold, dark, nothing ran through me. The following hours and days felt like someone hit fast forward and when my life resumed, it was over.

I wish I would've stopped for a minute and allowed myself the time to process. Instead, I was selfish and acted hastily. I was concerned with how this would affect my future and how I wasn't strong enough to endure the path that lay ahead.

Anyone going through something of that caliber should have to go through rigorous counseling. I needed someone to sit with me while I sat with everything that just happened. I needed prayer and to be pointed back to Jesus. Honestly, He's the only one I might've listened to.

Although I don't remember much about the conversation or even how I found the clinic, I made the call and scheduled the appointment. My mom supported my decision and agreed to be there with me even though it probably destroyed her.

Some may argue that I was justified in doing what I did and to be honest, it's sometimes hard to argue with. Everyone has their own walk with God and I am not using this as a platform to shame other women who have experienced similar situations. For me though, justified or not, the decision I made to have an abortion has haunted me forever.

Yes, I would've carried inside me the baby of my assailant, and I might've spent the rest of my life struggling emotionally, mentally and otherwise. BUT, the baby was also half mine; he was created in the image of God and for a purpose. My anger and fear prevented me from ever knowing or holding my own baby. I've had to spend my life knowing that I was someone capable of taking the life of her own child. The weight of that is extremely heavy and no amount of counseling or prayer can erase that from my heart. Although I now know I am forgiven for my iniquities, the reality and memory of what I did remains.

The irony is that I didn't believe I was strong enough to handle the complexity and emotions of having a child in that way, but I have never been stronger or felt more capable as a woman than I did when becoming a mother.

Immediately after my abortion I felt heartbroken and deeply saddened. I told myself it was in the past and tried to move forward, eventually "letting it go". Or so I thought. Any memory of that day or mention of abortion would quickly trigger me and I would start crying. Despite the circumstances that led me there, I couldn't help but be reminded of the weight of my sin and face the reality of what I had done.

It's nearly impossible to fit my experience into a short paragraph but during my Bible study I wrote a poem that summarized the pain as black and white as it felt.

One heart, beating fast

A child of God

First breath to last

Feeling scared and all alone

Curled up in her bed at home

Walking the path but feeling lost

Unaware of what it'd cost

One heart, beating fast

A child of God

Taken way too fast

Swan Song

Realizing I had been raped didn't happen until long after the incident. I specifically remember discussing that night with my mom and when she asked if I had been raped, I quickly replied "No, but I was taken advantage of" Had I been completely honest with her and shared every detail, she wouldn't have had to ask.

It wasn't until I shared everything with a group of women I just met, that I was faced with the reality. As I started to share my story, one of the women spoke up without hesitation and said "You were raped!" I paused for a minute and looked at her, feeling like someone just dropped a bomb on me. Throughout the course of the Bible study I soon began to realize that she was right. Rape isn't limited to the kind of experience where a woman is thrown to the ground, screaming "No!" as the abuser forces himself on her. If the woman is unconscious or unable to reason, it's still rape, and it's still traumatizing.

I couldn't believe that I had gone so long refusing to admit the truth and that it took a stranger to make me see that. Going through the necessary but painful Bible study, I realized how lax I had been in *attempting* to recover from what I had been through. It wasn't until I heard the words uttered from someone else's mouth, that I *truly* heard them. Until I heard someone else voice it, I didn't realize the gravity of the situation or the weight I carried around for so many years.

Thinking back to that naive woman, I can't believe how blind I was. It's amazing that when you experience trauma, your brain has the ability to shield you from any memory of it. Unfortunately, my memory was only blurred and only for so long. There are stages of every emotion we go through whether it's anger, grief or healing. In navigating my path to healing, I uncovered a lot of hurt that I didn't know existed or forgot was even there. I began to experience new emotions about an experience that happened over a decade ago: feeling pain that I pushed down, confronting anger that I never dealt with, and sadness that I didn't allow myself to feel.

Subconsciously I knew what happened that night. It was too painful to label my situation as rape but that's exactly what it was. Choosing to believe I was taken advantage of versus being raped seemed like the better, safer choice. Little did I know how negatively the semantics would affect me. Not only had I been walking around feeling the shame of an abortion, but I spent all those years blaming myself again and again. Thinking that I allowed that to happen only fueled hatred for myself. Thus, the root of my "unworthy" complex.

Already facing the heartbreak of my abortion, I was then discovering I was raped. My emotions were in overdrive and I sometimes struggled to breathe thinking about all the baggage I was carrying. I kept thinking about the fact that not only was I a murderer, but I was also raped. Honestly, I couldn't decide which trauma to focus on; the choice to end my child's life or the complete invasion of my mind and body.

Equally surprising to me, because I had never even considered it, was the question of whether or not I had been drugged prior to being raped. Again, a woman in our Bible study was the one who inquired about that possibility. I answered honestly and said that I had never even thought of that. Blaming myself as harshly as I did, I was blinded to anything other than me being irresponsible.

Unable to shake the feeling that most of the night was black, leading up to and including the rape, I decided to research date-rape drugs and their symptoms. Soon after completing my search, I found all the answers I needed. Several pieces of the puzzle began to fall into place and that once fuzzy night, became a little clearer. Date-rape drugs have the capability of making someone who is usually reserved, behave more sexually. The physical side effects also mimic those of a hangover so if a woman has been drinking, she wouldn't think twice.

I hated myself for so long thinking about how physically forward I was with him. The only memory that was clear in my mind was the fact that I had been very flirtatious with him. Considering how little I liked the guy, I couldn't understand why I would've behaved that way towards him, especially in a group setting.

It was uncharacteristic and the only explanation I could give was that I drank too much. Unfortunately, I drank often enough to know that I *never* behaved like that or blacked out as a result of drinking too much. I was always lucid enough to be aware of unsafe situations and say no when I was uncomfortable. Since I didn't know any better, I quickly blamed myself for over-drinking and essentially "asking for it". Neither of those are an excuse for what he did but nevertheless, I blamed myself for being in such a position in the first place. That is, until I began to realize I had no control over any of that.

I felt violated in a whole new way. It feels like such an invasion to alter someone's physical and mental state, just to leave them questioning their own judgement. For years I have been so angry with myself for "drinking too much" and acting inappropriately. It made me rethink every decision I ever made and hate myself for being so negligent.

Realizing now that I was most likely drugged, I am mourning all those years that I questioned my worthiness. I relinquished a lot of the blame on his part because I couldn't help but think that it was a result of my reckless behavior.

That makes me angry with him in a whole new way. I was simply sharing some drinks with a friend and I thought I was safe. I never would have guessed that I was about to be the victim of a horrible event that would lead me to such heartbreak. One drink changed my entire life. One night changed me forever.

It is the strangest thing to feel like you *just* learned about something unspeakable that happened to you over a decade ago. You were there and you lived it but from an entirely different mindset;

convinced that one thing happened when in reality, it was an entirely different situation that is even worse than the one you've been grieving.

Now, several years after the fact, I am learning so much about myself and what I truly experienced. How could I have gotten it so wrong? How could I have been so naive and quick to blame myself for something that was so clearly out of my control?

From the moment I woke up the next morning, I blamed myself. I blamed myself for putting myself in that position. I blamed myself for my behavior and how it led to the outcome of that night. I blamed myself for letting someone take advantage of my vulnerability.

Discovering new information about what actually happened unlocked so many new emotions. I am angry in a way that I wasn't before, angry in a way that people have told me I *should* be. I feel much more empathy for my younger self and the traumatic experience I went through. I'm incredibly sorry that I was so hard on myself for what happened *to* me. I just wish I could have shown myself grace, the way I now know God has shown me grace.

Going through the Bible study ended up being a realization, as well as a recovery. I was forced to come face-to-face with what I had experienced, as well as begin to heal from what I had done to resolve the "problem".

For over twelve years I carried around this painful secret. While a handful of people knew about the abortion, no one knew what truly happened the night I got pregnant. It wasn't until I went through the Bible study that I realized my husband didn't even know the full truth. He was always so supportive of my decision to abort and I always thought that was why; that he believed my decision was valid because of the rape. His support wasn't based on reasoning or justification. It was purely out of love; he didn't need to know why.

Uncovering the truth, however, lit a fire inside my husband. Rightfully so, he was angry with the man who did that to me and heartbroken to think of how many other victims there were. Going through my healing journey, we both struggled to compartmentalize our feelings about everything I went through. I didn't want to derail my healing from one trauma by focusing on the other, but I ignored both for far too long.

When I shared with my husband that I forgave everyone involved in my story but myself, he told me that was only because I never really admitted what happened. As part of the Bible study, we were forced to face our anger and address those who had hurt us in writing. Before I sat down to write the letter, I could still only think of the anger I harbored for myself. Once the pen hit the paper however, I realized I had many things to be angry about.

"To the 'Father',

For a long time I have pushed my feelings down and ignored all the pain and anger and confusion of that night twelve years ago. I've made excuses for you, as well as myself.

I regret ever having come to your house and putting myself in a position that gave you any kind of control over me or my body. For you it was just one night; a night that you probably never thought about again, a night that didn't cause you any heartbreak or counseling to recover from. For me on the other hand, it was just one of many days filled with regret

and shame and anger, a night that changed the course of my path and made me question my worthiness in the eyes of the Lord.

You weren't there when I nervously took a test or when I hastily made a decision based on fear and confusion and hurt. You weren't there when I dodged hateful looks and hurtful protests. You weren't there when I sat alone in a room filled with nothing but fear and anxiety, as I closed my eyes to avoid further heartbreak. You weren't there the days following when I was curled up under the covers with even more confusion and hurt. And you haven't been there any moment since as I've struggled to pick up the pieces and deal with this life-altering decision. You've gone on living your life without a single thought of that fateful night while I've questioned my very being and whether or not I'd ever find forgiveness, from myself or God. And you are the one who put me in that position.

What makes me even more angry is that I think I already have forgiven you, before I've even forgiven myself. That kind of grace is what God has taught me though and going through this experience has brought me closer to him. In a few short paragraphs, this angry letter has turned into my "swan song". The part of me that was angry and shameful about that night has died.

From now on, anything I wrestle with will be between myself and the Lord, my God. I have no space left in my heart to feel anything towards you and I pray that God shows you the same compassion.

Good bye."

I kept thinking that sharing my story would be the most difficult part of this journey; exposing myself to a group of women that were once strangers, trying to keep my composure long enough to get the words out. While writing down and speaking the words out loud was incredibly difficult for me, it was just the tip of the iceberg. Everything that followed is what truly broke me.

Where There's A Will

Once I was able to face and say goodbye to my anger towards the man that wronged me, I could focus on the child that changed me. Afterall, that was the reason for my brokenness. I can forgive someone who has hurt me but it truly breaks my heart to know that I was responsible for taking someone's life.

Anytime adoption was mentioned, I would quickly respond by saying there was no way I would be able to give up my own child. Instead I chose to take their life away. The irony of that is not lost on me and it destroys me to think that I chose that as an alternative. Even if what I experienced was a sin, taking life is also a sin, and just like my situation, my baby was not in control. They were innocent.

"I pray that I may grieve not only what I didn't choose but also what I did. I don't want to write off what I did as "acceptable" just because I didn't choose it. I am not the victim." - a prayer I wrote while going through my Bible study journey

Some could argue that carrying a baby for nine months and feeling them move inside of you bonds the two of you in a way eight short weeks cannot. While that may be true, miscarriages often happen on the same timeline and are equally damaging. The bottom line is that saying goodbye to a life that once lived inside of you, no matter how long, is tragic.

Honestly, what I experienced prior to their conception is beside the point. God had a plan for their life from conception to birth and their days were prepared before even living one day. They are formed inside the mother's womb by the Creator himself.

For you formed my inward parts; you knitted me together in my mother's womb. I praise you, for I am fearfully and wonderfully made. Wonderful are your

works; my soul knows it very well. Psalm 139: 13-14

Facing the truth was almost unbearable. While it had been slowly eating away at me for years, bringing it to light was devastating in a whole new way. A large piece of me had been living in the dark, away from God. I didn't believe He could forgive me for taking the life of one of His own so I kept it a secret as if I could hide it from Him.

Knowing nothing is ever hidden from our maker, it was no secret. Still, by not voicing it and keeping it hidden from everyone else, I convinced myself it never happened. That kind of life-altering decision should never be taken so lightly. Understandably, it's not something you want to shout from the rooftop, but I believe bringing light to what I did paved the way for true repentance. I had to face the reality that I did something truly "unforgiveable" to be able to believe I was already forgiven.

I prayed about it time and time again but my prayers were only seeking forgiveness for what I had done rather than asking for help to heal and allowing Him to do so. Confessing my sins was the first step in addressing the problem, but I also needed to be reminded of our great God and the beauty of His grace.

Something told me years ago that the baby was a boy, although it was too early to know for sure. I declined to see him or know anything about him before they took him. While in the Bible study and writing a letter to him, God revealed to me that his name was Will. After closing my journal and deciding to finish the letter another time, the name Will hit me out of nowhere and I just knew. I knew that his name was a sweet reminder that while we don't see the path God has for us, it *is* His will. I didn't plan to get pregnant but that doesn't mean it wasn't supposed to happen: God doesn't make mistakes.

As if knowing his name wasn't already incredibly surreal, I calculated his possible due date and the day that I sat down to write his letter, would've been his twelfth birthday. My entire body covered in goosebumps, I couldn't help but smile and cry thinking of him. Equally sweet, I had a vision of him and he looked like an older version of our then five-year-old. Same face and contagious smile, as well as the same gentle demeanor; a boy of few words but the absolute best heart.

I thought in giving more identity to the child I chose to give up, I would feel more pain, but I actually felt an overwhelming sense of happiness. Knowing that not only had God forgiven me but both He and my baby were watching over me and loving me was surreal and unbelievably touching; unconditional love at its finest.

As I sit and type up the letter I wrote to him almost a year ago, I can only write one sentence at a time. Each line pierces me deeply but also comforts me in a weird way. Even my husband said that reading it gave him a feeling of happiness. I truly never thought that thinking of him would bring me any emotion other than regret or sorrow, but now I am able to celebrate him and his meaningful life. I can rest easy knowing he's in good hands.

"Baby Will,

You were created by a good, good God. You were knit together in my womb and seen by God. I did not know your story or

our Heavenly Father is the only solace I have.

Learning more about God's grace and His love for all His children, I feel I am forgiven for my sins, namely the decision to end your life. The reality of that will NEVER be forgotten and a piece of my heart will always reside with you in Heaven.

I find comfort in knowing my heart will be full when we meet again and I have a chance to hold you, this time in my arms. Although it's hard to believe I deserve it, I feel your love and your presence here with me today, on what would've been your twelfth birthday.

Please know that I love you too and that all my fear, anger and pain from this journey is directly related to the piece of me that was broken when we were torn apart.

I loved you then, I love you now and I will love you forever. You are my son and more importantly God's son. While our journey together here on earth was just a short time, our time together in Heaven will be eternal.

Until we meet again my sweet boy,

Mama"

The Weight Of It All

I was so consumed by how horrible I felt
and how poorly I acted as a "devout"
Christian that I completely missed the
point. Our Lord and Savior is ten times
more amazing than our worst mistakes.

How could I be so naive to think that
the one who created me, in His own image,
could ever think of me as unworthy? Just
by believing that, I was not only doubting,
but disrespecting my own Creator. It was
selfish of me to only be considering how *I*
felt and how my decisions would impact
me. The Lord God had shown me grace
and instead of accepting His merciful gift, I
questioned whether or not it was meant
for me.

I didn't understand two very important things. This life we have and the grace bestowed upon us, is a gift. We did nothing to earn it. Also, we are meant to appreciate that gift and share its beauty with others, not burden ourselves with what we did to deserve it.

Shame on me for disregarding an important lesson we were taught as children; if someone is generous enough to give you a gift, you kindly accept and thank them for their thoughtfulness. You don't throw it in their face, demanding they got it wrong.

Often people assume that by believing in and praying to God you are relinquishing all heartbreak and turmoil. That if He exists, nothing life-shattering should ever happen to you or anyone you love. In theory, that would be amazing and hard to argue with but it would also be extremely easy, which nothing worth having is. Having faith doesn't excuse us from the pangs of the world, it simply gives us hope that with Him, we can make it through. It also puts into perspective the time and manner with which we live on earth. Believing in our mighty Creator and all He has granted us reminds us not only of His power but also how there is infinitely more beyond this world.

The same concept goes for having bad days. While they seem impossibly long and difficult to recover from, they are but a fraction of our time on earth and even *more* insignificant to what lies ahead. We're quick to label days as "bad" but it is often just a bad moment, something that probably won't matter come tomorrow. All this to say that we will experience rough days, weeks, even years, but by believing in Him, we can rest easy knowing that this isn't it. He is far greater than anything we go through and there is far more in store for us.

With that being said, He wants us to value the time we have here. We've been given this amazing opportunity to experience his glory and share it with everyone we come across.

I've always been one of those who believed whole-heartedly in the glory and power of the Holy Spirit and the presence in our lives; that something much bigger than all of us could intervene and perform miracles in the name of our King.

Admittedly, I was also one of those that ignored the other half of the equation; that with the spirit of good and holy working in our lives, there is also a spirit of evil working against us. Turning a blind eye to the existence of supreme evil and the stronghold it can have on our every move.

After experiencing pain and sorrow for as long as I did, I am aware now more than ever, the grasp the devil can have on us. Appearing subtle at times and often mistaken as the voice inside our heads, he is able to convince us of all the lies we don't want to believe. Once he is able to break down our walls and play to our emotions, it's not long before he has the power to make us question God himself. The second we begin to question our very Creator, the easier it is to lose sight of our worth and purpose.

Those all consuming thoughts that whisper "You only have yourself to blame" and "How could you?!" are coming straight from the devil himself and are all part of his plan to destroy us in our walk with God. He knows that should we discover the beauty of God's grace, deceiving us will be much more difficult. Not impossible, but requiring a lot more effort.

Never did I see my struggle with guilt and shame as an act of defiance. I wasn't questioning whether or not He could forgive us for our sins. The problem was, and still is sometimes, with my ability to forgive myself. By refusing to forgive myself however, I was unable to accept His grace. Without realizing it, I had begun to question the level of sin that could be forgiven. I thought my sin was bigger than Him, that what I had done made me unworthy of His grace.

We must build up our walls and strengthen our armor to defend ourselves against the devil's constant ploy to diminish our confidence, hope and faith. God is far greater than the worst of our sins. He is the almighty and we are His children, worthy of all the love He has bestowed upon us.

But God shows his love for us in that while we were still sinners, Christ died for us. Romans 5:8

I was living in a state of shame for so long that I began to believe I wasn't worthy. For so long I missed out on living abundantly because I was weighed down by my guilt and self-hatred. Instead of handing my pain and anger over to Him, I kept myself hidden. I turned my back on the only one who could truly heal me.

Our Story In The Stars

Our family sold our home and moved out of state to Arizona when our oldest two were under three. We'd always envisioned packing up and moving somewhere new in the spirit of adventure and a change of scenery.

Six months in, we found out we were pregnant with our third baby. A couple days after we found out, we were driving to Colorado to visit our family, so we chose to tell them in person. I was only seven weeks along but we didn't want to share it over the phone and we were too excited to wait. We spent the next few days on a high from sharing our pregnancy news and being surrounded by family. Just one week later, back in Arizona, we lost our baby.

I suspected it that morning because of my symptoms but I didn't want to believe it. I spent the afternoon alone in the bathroom until my husband got home from work. The kids were napping so I sat on the bathroom floor and cried, unable to process what just happened. Seeing the tiny little fetus that was growing inside me just one day earlier, I couldn't bring myself to flush the toilet. "This is my baby. How am I supposed to pull the lever and watch him or her literally go down the drain?"

Carrying a human inside you and seeing just how tiny and intricate they are at that stage is surreal. It makes you think of how amazing our Creator really is and also, how fragile life is. What begins as just a seed, soon grows to fill your arms.

When my husband got home, we cried and prayed over our baby together before saying goodbye. Although, we could've spent several days in that bathroom together and no amount of time would've felt sufficient enough to say goodbye to our child.

The days following were incredibly emotional for several reasons; we had just experienced one of the most tragic losses you can imagine, I was away from all our family and most of our friends, and blamed myself for losing the baby.

I know that God doesn't send us tragedy as a form of punishment for our past but that is exactly what went through your purpose but God did, he knew every chapter and it was beautifully written.

It was not my plan to be your mother but it *was* God's will. We make mistakes but he does not. I will never know what your story was or the life he had planned for you.

Although you never lived a day apart from me and your life on earth was short, it was powerful and life-changing. It was my job to help you grow but as it turns out, you actually helped *me* to grow. Your life showed me that God has a plan for our lives and what that holds is beyond our comprehension or control.

I understand now that God knows what is best and even if we don't see the purpose, we are better off walking the path with him rather than creating our own.

I have cried many tears over the prospect of what your life and our lives together could've been. I've wondered what would've become of the life I destroyed. Knowing that you are beside Jesus with my mind. The moment I realized what was happening, I immediately started blaming myself and thought "I had this coming. Had I never chosen to give up my baby, I wouldn't be losing this one now."

For the record, my past had absolutely nothing to do with it. Women experience this kind of loss daily and it has nothing to do with anything they did or didn't do. It happens. There is no explanation and no preparation. Likewise, it doesn't matter how many children you already have or how far along you are, losing a baby is losing a baby.

Growing life inside of you is a miracle and to grieve the loss of such is as painful as it is beautiful.

Blaming myself for the loss of our baby prevented me from truly grieving. I didn't allow myself the time to properly heal because I kept telling myself that my miscarriage was inevitable. Truthfully, I think I partially expected it with every pregnancy, before the loss and especially after.

After moving back home and surrounding ourselves with family once again, there was a sense of belonging but a piece was missing. I felt as though we left our baby there; moving home and moving on without her. That time in our lives will always be an adventure but as that chapter came to an end, so did one of our sweet babies.

We have since named our sweet baby
Story and her name is a reminder that
while she is not here with us, she will
always be a part of our story.

"Sweet baby,

**You've already been missing from my
belly for longer than the time I knew you
existed. That thought kills me. You were
unexpected but we were so grateful for
you; unplanned but SO wanted.
My whole body aches when I think of
what we lost; a tiny little baby, a sibling
for our children, a lifetime of memories. I
truly feel the pain of losing you, in every
way and in every bone. A phrase by the
way, I hate to use. We didn't lose you, we
know exactly where you are. You are in
God's hands, an angel among the angels.
Knowing you for just a short time and
feeling your presence within me, has
changed me forever. You will always be**

my third child and you will never be forgotten.

For whatever God has planned, our paths were not meant to cross in the physical world but I am beyond happy to see what He has planned for us in Heaven. Our souls will reunite and once again be bonded by the unbroken connection between a mama and her baby.

Until we meet again my sweet child,

Your Mama, forever."

Learning we were pregnant again after the miscarriage was a bittersweet moment. My initial reaction was pure happiness, immediately followed by fear. I couldn't help but feel completely anxious by my many emotions. I was of course, so grateful that God had blessed us with a baby yet again but I was also so nervous to experience the same outcome.

Although I wanted to feel excited and hopeful for the future, I prevented myself from thinking about our baby too much. I was so terrified for so long that I couldn't experience the beauty of pregnancy as I should have. It was heartbreaking trying to avoid the happiness that comes with growing a life inside of you.

Immediately following the birth of our third (earthside) baby, I hemorrhaged. I gave birth naturally following a cesarean and the doctor didn't take the correct precautions to ensure I didn't bleed. I laid there, unmedicated, in excruciating pain as the team of doctors and nurses rushed in and performed every possible measure to stop it. Focusing on the newborn baby lying on my chest, I attempted to distract myself from the intense pain. Every time I opened my eyes, I could see the look in both my husband and mom's eyes and their reactions only scared me more. My mom confessed later that she had worried our baby boy might lose his mother before he even had a chance to know me. My husband told me when we left the hospital that he didn't want us to have any more children. He was truly scarred. They both were.

They were traumatized and I couldn't even relate. While it was incredibly painful and traumatizing for me as well, it was in a different way. My eyes were closed and I shut out the world to protect myself and my new baby. It wasn't *me* who stood there watching in horror as my worst fears played out in front of me. To this day, discussing the birth still brings tears to our eyes.

Refusing at first to even consider more children, my husband tried to explain just how painful the birth was to witness. Reasonably so, he didn't want to bring another baby into the world if it meant all of them could lose their mother. When my husband has a very strong opinion on something, I try not to ignore his intuition. He is someone who is extremely easy going and rarely angered or upset; one of the things I love most about him.

Despite our fears, we decided to let God decide what the plan for our growing family would be. He blessed us with one more baby girl two years later, almost to the day. We are so incredibly grateful to have her as our youngest and that we let God choose our fate.

Losing our child was heartbreaking and affected me on so many levels for so many reasons. I am grateful however, that we were able to experience the beauty of bringing two more babies into the world afterwards. God gifted us with their health, as well as mending a piece of our brokenness.

Despite my iniquities, God has blessed me again and again and I am eternally and unfathomably grateful.

In The Shadows

While I was pregnant with our rainbow baby, our dog's health significantly declined and we had to put him down.

Nash was gifted to me as a puppy and I raised him and loved him for almost thirteen years. He saw me through breakups and heartaches and the pregnancies of our first two children. The week before we lost our baby, I witnessed him experience his first seizure as a result of his diabetes and it was heartbreaking. Following our return from Arizona, his health and quality of life diminished and we decided it was time to say goodbye. I absolutely hated that I had to play God and choose when his "time" was. It brought back painful memories of my decision to abort my baby and the responsibility to make that call felt crushing.

That same month, on Christmas Eve, one of our closest friends and best man at our wedding, took his own life. Watching my husband lose his childhood best friend in such a traumatic way is something I wouldn't wish on anyone.

In the early days of our relationship, he, my husband and I spent a lot of time together. We went on many adventures and trips together and I was grateful to have known him. I think often about his speech at our wedding because as sweet as it was then, it is even more meaningful now. "I was worried that when my best friend got married, I'd lose a best friend but instead, I gained one." We truly loved him and all the ways he brought people together.

Saying goodbye to loved ones was becoming all too familiar and I was at my breaking point. Some days, the tiny life growing inside me was all that kept us together. Him, and our other young children who needed us to be present and hopeful. We couldn't afford to check out. One of the most difficult times of our lives and marriage was going through that season of heartbreak.

My husband has sadly gone through the loss of many people, several being friends of his. Even more unfortunate, this wasn't the first he had lost to suicide. Suicide is one of those topics that people don't truly understand until they have lost someone close to them. It's easy to have an opinion on something you have never been through: suicide, rape and abortion being a few. Often labeled as selfish, suicide is extremely hard to understand as an outsider. With most traumatic experiences, the person going through them rarely shares the depth of their pain. There are things that even close friends and family never knew and might not ever learn.

The year my husband and I got engaged, we went to the funeral of a childhood friend's husband. They hadn't been married long and she was understandably devastated. Being a witness to someone saying goodbye to their spouse so young was absolutely agonizing and at the time it was the hardest funeral I ever had to attend. That is until we lost our best friend to suicide at such a young age. Trying to make sense of his choice to end his own life nearly destroyed us.

In the same way, losing our baby was confusing and a test to our faith. No matter how you lose someone, the pain is the same. There is nothing you can do to lessen the pain of saying goodbye to a loved one and there is nothing anyone else can say to console you in the moment. Despite the promise of the paradise that lies beyond the grave, losing someone to the only world you know is crushing.

Dealing with death is handled in many different ways, as is trauma.

The Lord is near to the brokenhearted and saves the crushed in spirit. Psalms 34:18

So many of us are desperately broken and don't even realize it. We've buried something so far down that we don't even remember the depth or severity of our wounds. My story held so much pain and had such a hold on me, yet I acted as though it never happened.

Until I had shared my story with the women in my Bible study, I could count on one hand the number of people I told. Still to this day, the majority of my family doesn't know what I have been through. I was so ashamed and so fearful of judgement that I chose to keep quiet.

Thinking about what I experienced and the years I secretly struggled, I feel for others who are going through the same. I no longer hold any judgment for how someone handles a situation or towards my own past. I know that God's opinion of me is the only one that matters and my walk with Him is personal, as is everyone else's.

Needless to say, that chapter of our lives really shook us. We went through some really low lows and really high highs. Losing loved ones but also welcoming new ones to our family. A lot of our healing was postponed and because of that, it took us a long time to recover and find peace in all the circumstances we were dealt. These are the moments that you have a choice to make. You can choose to be consumed by your pain and sorrow or use it to shape you into someone who is stronger, grateful and more present. Many times the thing that nearly breaks us, is actually the thing that builds us up.

But he said to me,"My grace is sufficient for you, for my power is made perfect in weakness." Therefore I will boast all the more gladly of my weaknesses, so that the power of Christ may rest upon me. For the sake of Christ, then, I am content with weaknesses,

insults, hardships, persecutions, and calamities. For when I am weak, then I am strong. 2 Corinthians 12:9-10

The Mountains Are Calling

The mountains are calling. This phrase has always been the most accurate description of what my heart desires. As a child, my Dad would take us skiing at a little resort in Colorado and even though I was the absolute worst skier, I insisted on going. Every time, he'd inquire "You don't like skiing, are you sure you want to go?" and every time without hesitation, I'd say "Yes, I want to go!" Later on, I discovered that I liked snowboarding much more, but either way, the true motivation was a trip to the mountains.

To this day, I desperately crave time in the mountains, even if just for the day and even if just for the view. When I need some time away to recharge, I'll grab a coffee and find a trailhead close by so I can look at the mountains while listening to music or journaling. I married someone with an equal love for the outdoors and we're now raising kids who'll request a "picnic with a view" and a weekend away in the mountains.

It's not surprising that when I'm struggling with something or needing an escape, my soul longs for something as majestic as the mountains. I think it's God's way of putting things in perspective; reminding us of the simplistic beauty of life and the world around us, and a reminder that our Creator is capable of amazing things. Breathing in fresh mountain air and soaking in the beauty of nature is all I need to reset.

Not only did my husband and I get engaged and married in the mountains, but I recently got baptised in the mountains for my fortieth birthday. After going through an incredible journey to heal and reconnect with God, I couldn't think of a better way to spend such a milestone. I was never baptized as a kid and although I've been a follower of Jesus for a long time, it felt more fitting now than ever before.

There are moments in your life that you know immediately will last in your mind and heart forever. Details will be etched in your memory and even when you're old and grey, that moment in time will feel like it just happened yesterday. Our wedding day and the birth of our four beautiful children are a few of those, as is my baptism.

The day was everything I needed and even more than I could've expected. Similar to most organized events in my life, the day itself was a little chaotic and there were a few surprises. Still though, it was absolutely perfect and if I could relive it again and again I would.

I decided earlier in the year that I wanted to be baptized by my uncle who is a Reverend and I wanted it to be done in the mountains. I woke up one morning and it hit me, like it had been chosen for me. Without hesitation, I told my husband, "I know how I want to celebrate my fortieth birthday. I want to be baptized in a river in the mountains" As fate would have it, my uncle was planning to be in Colorado the week of my birthday and he happily accepted my request to baptize me.

Per usual, the Colorado weather was unpredictable and as expected, more than one of our children were crying but as soon as I stepped into the water, everything was calm. Even as I lowered my body into the freezing water and my body began to tremble, I felt oddly at peace. The only thing I could think about was how much this meant to me and how I was going to remember this moment, right here, for the rest of my life.

Our little babes spent the morning searching for and picking all the dandelions they could find "Because you're getting baptized", they told me as they excitedly raised each one up to my face with a smile. Our family started to arrive and with each person that walked up, I felt more and more blessed. Blessed for what I was about to experience, blessed for so many people I love being a witness, and blessed for where my path led me.

I stood there and listened to the words my uncle, Gary was speaking and I was torn between wanting to smile and holding back tears. Looking at everyone standing around us, I saw how each of them made some impact on my life and the decisions that led me there that day. I graciously replied "I do" and "I will" as prompted, thinking about how two simple words can hold so much weight and mean so much. Almost ten years earlier, I repeated those same two words when reciting vows to my husband less than a hundred feet from that very spot on the river.

Now, several years later and with our children as a witness, I was making one of the most important decisions you can make in life. After being a Christian for forty years, I was finally able to accept the beauty of His grace and choose Jesus, just as He had chosen me.

Why, even the hairs of your head are all numbered. Fear not; you are of more value than many sparrows. Luke 12:7

No matter what you've been through or how big your sins are, nothing should keep you from turning to Jesus. Keeping yourself from Him because you feel unworthy would only mean He died for nothing. He did that for you.

Accepting you are worthy of the kind of love only God can give is both difficult and beautiful. If I'm being honest, I'm not sure I ever really believed I was worthy until I faced the reality that I did something "unworthy".

Now I'm Found

After going through a long and painful journey to reunite with God, I found myself again. I know who I am and more importantly what He has called me to do. I believe with all my heart that I was meant to get lost and lose my way so that I could truly understand what it means to be found; relating so much to the lost sheep and wanderer of the story who needed my shepherd to help guide me home.

What man of you, having a hundred sheep, if he has lost one of them, does not leave the ninety-nine in the open country, and go after the one that is lost, until he finds it? And when he has found it, he lays

it on his shoulders, rejoicing. And when he comes home, he calls together his friends and his neighbors, saying to them "Rejoice with me, for I have found my sheep that was lost." Just so, I tell you, there will be more joy in heaven over one sinner who repents than over ninety-nine righteous persons who need no repentance. Luke 15:4-7

The Lord took my hand and led me back to the only path I'll ever need to walk; the one that may be rocky and dark but will without a doubt, lead me to the light. Despite my repeated mistakes and what seemed like deliberate attempts to ignore His calls, He never left my side. He nudged me back to where I was supposed to be, leading me back to my husband and what would become the best of many decisions to come. Not long after, He blessed us four times over with the gifts of our four healthy, happy children.

After going through the process to heal, I found Him yet again and on the deepest level. Still, it is a decision I have to make every day; to choose Him and His path over any others that may appear in the fog of choices before me. We must not get distracted by our struggles, current situations or the monotony of our daily lives. We have to focus on the importance of our time here on earth and what God has intended for our lives and the people we're entrusted to lead.

My eyes are fixed on Jesus and I don't ever want to stray again. Knowing full well that I will stumble and make mistakes but also knowing that I will never look back and question if I'm going in the right direction. Walking towards Jesus will never lead you to a place you're not meant to be. God has a plan for us all and if we put our trust in Him, we will not be disappointed.

I am the way and the truth and the life. John 14:6

I have this strong sense of belonging like never before and I know that as my father, the Lord God is proud of who I am but also expects me to take accountability for my actions. I am in no way releasing myself from my life of sin, but instead choosing repentance and choosing to use my story as a way to help others find God. I have finally accepted His grace wholeheartedly without letting my guilt or shame prevent me from living the life He imagined. He wanted that for me, for us.

While I believe that I sinned in a way that changed me forever, I now believe that I have been forgiven and there is something oddly comforting about admitting you are imperfect in your walk with Jesus. It humbles you and reminds you of your desperate need for Him in your life. I feel a more intimate connection with God and am grateful for the journey that brought me here.

Just like the Japanese art of kintsugi, my brokenness has been made beautiful. Breathtaking pieces of art are created by filling cracks in pottery with powdered gold. The result is a masterpiece, unveiling what can be made when our "cracks" are healed and made whole.

I will extol you, O Lord, for you have drawn me up and have not let my foes rejoice over me. O Lord my God, I cried to you for help, and you have healed me. Psalm 30:1-2

If I had to lose my way to find God, I am grateful for everything I've been through. Every heartbreak and mistake, every fall and wrong turn, were all worth it to find him again. I will forever be grateful that God brought me from the lowest of lows to the ultimate high.

There is truly no greater feeling than standing in worship, tears rolling down your face, in awe of this life you've been given. God is the only one who can pull you out of the darkest corners of the earth and place you on the tallest mountain. That feeling of absolute peace, freedom and gratitude is the work of God.

He has delivered us from the domain of darkness and transferred us to the kingdom of his beloved Son, in whom we have redemption, the forgiveness of sins. Colossians 1:13-14

By The Grace

Some days I still struggle to breathe thinking about what I have done. This healing journey has been long and painful and beautiful, all at the same time.

Oddly though, I am grateful for the continual healing. It reminds me just how amazing our God is. I did this horrible, earth shattering thing, and yet he still shows me grace. Being reminded of that kind of love over and over again helps to put things in perspective and keeps me grounded in my faith.

For by grace you have been saved through faith. And this is not your own doing; it is the gift of God. Ephesians 2:8

This verse is what finally made me realize that despite our iniquities, we are forgiven through our faith. We did nothing to earn this and no amount of sin can take it away.

Whether or not I was *worthy* wasn't the question. All I needed to ask myself was whether or not I believed that Jesus died for our sins. I did, I do, and I will continue to believe that for the rest of my days. That knowledge runs deep in my soul and it is the foundation for which I've built my faith. I believe in everything God has done and offered, giving up *His* own child to do so.

John 3:16 is the most quoted verse in the bible and with good reason. It embodies all we need to know about what Jesus did for us thousands of years ago and how deeply God loves us.

For God so loved the world, that he gave his only Son, so that whoever believes in him should not perish but have eternal life. John 3:16

By believing, repenting and accepting His grace, I have been saved. The faith I had as a child has been restored. Childlike innocence is something to be protected. We cannot be ignorant to the ways of our world but I believe we need to shut out all the noise so as not to miss God's voice. He speaks to us in many ways and the Holy Spirit surrounds us.

So put away all malice and all deceit and hypocrisy and envy and all slander, Like newborn infants, long for the pure spiritual milk, that by it you may grow up into salvation. 1 Peter: 1-2

Many times throughout my journey, I believe the Holy Spirit was there speaking through me. Much of what I journaled, the letters I wrote and the prayers I said, felt out of my hands. The words seemed to find the paper in a way that just flowed out of me. God is using us to speak his truth and reach everyone who is desperately searching for a voice. A voice to guide them in a world of chaos, a voice to show them the light in the darkest of our days.

Listening to the sermons each week, I am reminded time and again how grateful I am for everything I've been through. Thinking about how good our God is and how appreciative I am that I can *finally* accept His grace. Not just in an eternal sense, but here on earth. The only thing better than the gift of God's grace, is being able to understand and appreciate it for what it is.

I feel this immense passion and responsibility to share my story in hopes of helping even *one* person, to see the beauty of what we've been given. I am no longer bound by my shame or pain, but liberated. If going through the experience I did has a silver lining, it is my strengthened relationship with Jesus and if God has a purpose for each of us here on earth, mine is to help others to achieve the same.

I've always been burdened by the weight of the world. Some people are blessed with this amazing calling to help the less fortunate and they have the ability and resources to do so. Questioning how I would ever be able to help others, I kept feeling as though I had nothing to give. Even after listening to a sermon about helping others through our experiences and stories, I still came up short. At the end of my Bible study however, I felt this pull to share everything I experienced and more importantly, where it has led me today.

To look at where I currently am on my journey with God, the positives far outweigh all the hurt and pain I went through to get here. From now on, I promise to set my eyes on Jesus and follow the path that God has set out before me. I pray that God will use me to help others experience what I have; an immense appreciation for the gift that we've been given and a passion to share that with all the children of God.

As each has received a gift, use it to serve one another, as good stewards of God's varied grace. 1 Peter 4:10

It is by the grace of God that I made it through this journey. It is by the grace of God that I am truly able to accept His love. And it is by the grace of God that I was transformed from hurting to healed, broken to blessed.

www.ingramcontent.com/pod-product-compliance
Lightning Source LLC
Chambersburg PA
CBHW051630120626
46551CB00014B/2013